EDISON

David Boyle has been writing about new ideas for more than a quarter of a century. He is co-director of the New Weather Institute, a fellow of the New Economics Foundation, has stood for Parliament and is a former independent reviewer for the Cabinet Office. He is the author of *Alan Turing, Scandal* and *Before Enigma,* as well as a range of other historical studies.
He lives in the South Downs.

EDISON
Shining a light

David Boyle

THE REAL PRESS
www.therealpress.co.uk

Published in 2017 by the Real Press and for kindle by Endeavour Press.
www.therealpress.co.uk
© David Boyle

ISBN (print) 978-1977597878

For Agatha
With love and admiration

Contents

Introduction

The Great Entrepreneur

"I never did a day's work in my life;
it was all fun."
Thomas Edison

Every age believes that they are in the middle of unprecedented change, both social and technological. In a sense, perhaps, they are. The twelfth century coped with the changes that followed as a result of the emergence of universities and gothic cathedrals, inflation and the economic impact of wind energy; the sixteenth century faced the implications of the cultural breakthroughs of the Renaissance, plus the arrival of syphilis and precious metals from the New World.

Our own day, so often held up as an example of accelerated change, faces the economic shifts that follow the IT revolution; but, for the developed world at least, there was a period which trumped them all: the aftermath of the Industrial Revolution, and the shift from a predominantly rural way of life to an urban one.

If you were born in the 1880s, you would have experienced this shift first-hand, driven as it was by the suffering from the agricultural depression in the 1870s, and the upheavals in Eastern Europe, which saw unprecedented migration to Western Europe and America — when up to a quarter of the population of England left the countryside.

You would have witnessed the introduction of electric light, the first motor cars, cinemas, gramophones, safety bikes, submarines and aeroplanes, and — if you managed to survive the trenches of the First World War — you would have had a good chance of seeing all those technologies reach their full flowering in the 1960s: the traffic on ten-lane highways, the monstrous ballistic missile submarines and supersonic jet airliners. By the end of your life, the world you lived in would have been unrecognisable to your grandparents, and probably also your parents.

Compared to the extraordinary technological shifts and upheavals of the 1880s — based in their own way on the invention of the electric telegraph in the 1840s — our own time is a tame snail's pace of change, and what is most amazing about that period of utmost acceleration is that one man, Thomas Alva Edison, could have provided the keys to unlock so many of those technological changes.

Edison won most of the inter-inventor struggles for dominance over the key turn-of-the-century developments, from the development of electric light, to the gramophone and moving pictures, not just because he captured the technological spirit of the age, but because he also developed a world-beating method.

His developments were not just in the 'headline' areas either — he played a leading role in perfecting the telephone, in electrifying cities, in developing manmade rubber, creating effective batteries to power submarines under water, and even advocating the use of electricity to execute murderers. All of them involved Edison's unique combination of knowhow, teamwork and methodology.

Edison was the main reason why American technology came to dominate the century that was to come. Crucially, he developed the modern industrial ethos of innovation, presiding over a series of famous laboratories, with trusted teams working to his inspiration, which became almost as famous as he was. Hence perhaps the epithet, which one newspaper foisted on him; 'the Wizard of Menlo Park'.

The truth about Edison is that he was never exactly a scientist, though he was fascinated by science. He emerged instead from the great tradition of brilliant, self-taught amateurs, the engineers and technologists who the entrepreneurial advocate Samuel Smiles immortalised in 1859, in his book *Self Help*. The lives Smiles recorded were not so much the pure scientists like Faraday or Ohm, but those who put scientific ideas into practical effect. Edison had managed the transition from newspaper vendor on the Midwest railroad of the USA to become one of the most famous inventors on the planet. Edison did not inherit greatness; he clutched at it and worked at it — not for its own sake, but because it was fun and he was fascinated by the challenge.

The late, great retail entrepreneur Anita Roddick used to say that entrepreneurs were not primarily motivated by money: often they were people who imagined the world differently. Edison was certainly that — from one problem to the next, he grappled with the bugs and challenges in search of practical knowledge and, when he made money, he reinvested it in doing what he loved most: experimenting and asking difficult questions.

What seems to differentiate Edison from most of us questioning human beings is that he asked the right questions over and over again: what kind of filament would work in an electric light if such a thing were possible; how could the telephone diaphragm sound more clearly? And he had the

supreme confidence in his own ability to answer
them.

1
Railroads

"She was always so true and so sure of me. And always made me feel I had someone to live for and must not disappoint."
Thomas Edison about his mother, Nancy

Thomas Alva Edison was born on 11 February 1847 in Milan, Ohio, then the second largest wheat shipping centre in the world (after Odessa). He always adored his mother; Nancy Edison was a schoolteacher, and this turned out to be critical in Thomas's development as a self-taught scientist. It was she, when he was seven, who took him away from school, furious with the teacher's description of her son as 'addled' - (he did not speak until he was four years old, like the historian Lord Macaulay).

Like so many pioneers, Edison did not thrive with conventional schooling, but his mother was a hard taskmaster and an inspiring teacher. It became clear that he had the ability — rather as

Alan Turing did in the following century — to intuit mathematical answers without having to work them out.

Great pioneers also benefit from the context into which they were born, and Edison was born at the right moment in history, and probably also the right place — on the edge of the civilised world in rural Ohio. One of his first memories was seeing three huge covered wagons outside their home in Milan, about to undertake the two-thousand-mile journey to California. He had been born only two years before the California Gold Rush.

Although Edison had his roots in the old world, he was also born at a crucial moment in the development of communications technology. Four years before his birth, the American portrait painter Samuel Morse sent the first message down the electric telegraph. Electricity had only recently been grasped by people like Faraday, Ohm, Ampere and Clerk Maxwell — all of them Europeans — but the development of the telegraph and the development of railways went hand in hand, and especially in the new, expanding United States, burgeoning with manifest destiny.

Later in his life, when people asked him about his background, Edison used to encourage the idea that he had been born into poverty. It wasn't true. His father James was in the lumber business and had been since he fled from Canada after supporting the losing rebels in the uprising against British rule in 1837, led by William Lyon Mackenzie, the mayor of Toronto. This meant that important books of philosophy and science were available to him at home and, by the age of nine, he was reading European philosophers in the original languages — plus David Hume's *History of England* and Edmund Gibbon's *Decline and Fall of the Roman Empire*.

By the age of thirteen, he was reading Thomas Paine. He was always, in a sense, a free-thinking radical. We have become used to the idea that entrepreneurs tend to be conservative people — it isn't always the case, and was certainly never true of Edison.

Young Edison, known in childhood as Alva, was always involved in experiments and confusions of various kinds. He tried to repeat scientific experiments that he had read about in the basement of his family home, after the Edisons moved to Port Huron. He is said to have burned down the barn in the same way. But his first escapades in the world of work were not as a scientist, though he always loved to experiment; they were as an entrepreneur.

From the earliest age, he was able to discern gaps in the market which he could fill, and, like most entrepreneurs, he became particularly adept as he got older at understanding that the best gaps to fill were those which were so specialist that only he could fill them.

The morning train left Port Huron in those days at 7am and took four hours to go the 63 miles to the heart of Detroit, and then went back again, getting home again at 9.30pm. At the age of thirteen, fresh from reading Paine, Edison applied for the job of newsboy on the train and got it, putting an abrupt end to his schooling, and also beginning what would be a lifetime's absence from home because of his incessant work schedules.

Even during his years of married life, through two marraiges, he used to stay away from home working, often all night, and bed down in the corner of his laboratory under his desk. From the moment he took the job selling papers, he was away, and making a living using his wits.

One of the stories he told about the cause of his famous deafness suggests that it started when the guard boxed his ears. The other story was more complicated. He had been delayed on a platform by a passenger and had to run to catch the train. He tripped and nearly fell, which could have killed him under the wheels, but the guard caught him by the ear and pulled him to safety.

Whatever the true origins for this affliction, he

said that he felt something snap inside, and he claimed much later that his deafness – which increased with age – made him able to perfect the telephone. He couldn't hear what everyone else could hear, so he would only be satisfied by something that was really clear. Clarity of sound was always his ideal.

Edison earned his money on commission from the sales of the papers, and the first entrepreneurial question he seemed to have asked himself was: why just newspapers? His day soon became complex. He would buy sweets before collecting his papers for the day, and would sell them on the train on the way out. Then, in the six hour turnaround wait in Detroit, he would spend his time in the library of the Young Men's Association, before selling the evening papers on the way back. Soon he was also selling butter and vegetables, and he had other boys working for him.

Then came the next question: why not produce his own newspaper especially for the journey? He began to write his own copy, putting in any snippets of news he heard — the telegraph offices at the railway stations were the way that news spread in those days in the Midwest — and he was offered part of an unused luggage car to do the setting and the printing. Soon he was producing

400 copies a week and he called it the *Grand Trunk Herald*. In the other space in the same truck, he set up a small travelling laboratory so that he could do experiments in his spare moments.

It was in April 1862 when his first big opportunity emerged. The American Civil War was at its height and Edison discovered from the telegraph operator at Port Huron that a major battle was being fought. This was the Battle of Shiloh and the confederate general Albert Johnson had been killed during a surprise attack on Ulysses Grant's Army of Tennessee. Here was a chance to make some real money, but to drum up demand for his paper, the passengers had to know the battle was going on.

The first task was to ask the station master at every station where they stopped to chalk up the basic news on the same blackboard where they put the train times. He couldn't do that himself, because he would be on the train, so he asked the friendly operator at Port Huron to do it for him and he promised him free magazines for a month if he agreed. Then he typeset a special issue on the train and, when he got to Detroit, he went to the only place capable of producing the quantities of newsprint he needed — the offices of the *Detroit Free Press*. Could they produce him one- thousand five-hundred copies on credit? They dismissed the teenager immediately so he barged in to see the editor. Wilbur Storey listened in silence, then he gave Edison a slip of paper and said: "Take that downstairs and you will get what you want."

Three of his boys helped him fold the copies which were ready before the train left again. Then the question was whether the operator had kept his word. To his great relief, there was a huge crowd at the first station and he sold a hundred copies at five cents each. At the next station, he sold two hundred copies at ten cents each and so on back to Port Huron. There, he managed to sell the remaining copies to a church full of people on his way home. His first outing as an entrepreneur was a huge success. It also inadvertently led him on to the next stage of his career.

Edison decided that the way to better himself further was to somehow become a telegraph operator. It so happened that an incident took place which allowed Edison to get the experience he needed. A train was backing in Mount Clemens and Edison could see a small child in the way on the tracks. He rescued the child in the nick of time and he turned out to be the son of the telegraph operator there. Gratefully, the operator offered to teach Edison how to use the machine of the age.

In Port Huron later, Edison was allowed to help

in the jewellery and stationery store, where he could also tinker around repairing locks. Through the night, he would practice taking down the news reports as he would need to do if he worked more formally. He was already fascinated by electronics and telegraphy. Even before his railway job, he had built a half-mile cable system to send messages to and from his friend's house. His first telegraphy job was as a night operator at Stratford Junction.

When a job came up at Port Huron Station, (and telegraphy jobs had a famously high turnover), he applied and got it. He was now sixteen and took advantage of the space downstairs at the railway station to do the experiments that he read about in *Scientific American*.

If you had enough experience as a telegrapher, tapping out Morse code at speed and being able to take it down, you were able to make a reasonable living. In the rapidly expanding railway and cable system that was stretching westwards across the USA, there were always opportunities for the bright and the young with no family ties. And if you were dismissed from one station, there was always the next.

The tentacles of Western Union and the other cable companies were opening up possibilities everywhere to the new breed of hard-drinking young telegraphers. Edison was soon one of them, an itinerant operator, specialising in night shifts so that he could have the days free to do experiments, which also occupied him during the dull time between messages.

If he lost his job, he moved on — and he did lose jobs. Maybe he missed his hourly call sign, designed to make sure he was awake, or maybe the sulphuric acid from an experiment would spill through the floor. On one occasion, he had rigged up a device that would send the hourly call signal to an alarm clock. He missed orders to stop an oncoming train, and ran to find the signalman, but couldn't find him. It was an agonising moment and the freight trains involved nearly had a head on collision. He was dragged before the line superintendent, who threatened him with prison and, during an interruption, he slipped away and back home to Port Huron.

Edison developed his own distinctive style of sending messages, as the key operators tended to. Edison's was extremely fast, almost impossible to take down except by the most experienced and expert telegraphists. He also had an imaginative way of facing down problems. On one occasion, when the ice flows had damaged the cable between Port Huron and Sarnia, he had a flash of inspiration of the kind he would manage to develop his whole life, and suggested sending Morse code messages with train whistles to get messages across the river.

The pattern of Edison's life was becoming set. He began to get by on just three or four hours sleep a night, so that he had ample time for his experiments. He could see opportunities emerging now that peace had been declared. By 1865 and the end of the civil war, he had graduated to Cincinnati, working for Western Union. Then Nashville, then Memphis.

In Memphis, he experienced race riots — this was the brief moment in history before the carpetbaggers, when black former slaves were elected to run the former slave states. He had been planning to emigrate to seek a fortune in Brazil, but something about the riot changed his mind at the last moment. Then it was clear that the future for an ambitious young man lay with the big cities on the east coast, and he went to Boston. On the way from Toronto, he was caught in a giant snow drift and his train arrived four days late. Once there, he faced the prospect of a test by the sceptical, not to say cynical, hard-drinking, hard-womanising, testosterone-fuelled culture of the top telegraphers in the west.

Without telling him, the other operators put him on to receiving messages from the fastest sender at the New York office, aware that every eye in the room was on him. The operator began to abbreviate, knowing that Edison would have to write it out in full. Edison managed to escape humiliation by breaking into the message and telling New York that their sender was sounding tired, suggesting he used the other foot to send. "This saved me," Edison wrote later.

Edison was not the womanising nor the hard-drinking type, but he enjoyed the culture of exchanged jokes down the line — he was always one for funny stories. In fact, it provided the pattern for his famous friendship with the pioneer industrialist Henry Ford. In any case, he had been accepted as one of the elite. It was just that he didn't intend to stay one — he had another route before him.

2
Telegraphs

"None of my inventions came by accident. I see a worthwhile need to be met and I make trial after trial until it comes. What it boils down to is one per cent inspiration and ninety-nine per cent perspiration."
Thomas Edison, 1903

By the late 1860s, Edison had fully mastered the complexities and techniques of the telegraph, but he also brought to it a new scientific knowledge and an inquiring mind. It was obvious to him which way the technology was going . What appeared to be the next innovation was a way of using the wires more efficiently by sending and receiving two messages on the same line at the same time. That was the duplex machine. Ever since his brief period in Memphis, he had been wondering how it might be possible to send messages simultaneously. He had begun to get involved in the technical development of private telegraphy. He had helped fit a private cable system in Cincinnati between the offices of the local soap and candle provider Procter and Gamble. He was already actively wiring people up.

But Edison began what was, in effect, his inventing career in Boston in 1868, where he was wrestling not just with the duplex problem, but with a range of other issues that interested him. It was always his technique to work on a range of problems at the same time, finding that this allowed him to take problems unawares, because, once he abandoned the question he was struggling with to work on something else, the solution sometimes popped into his head.

It was a problem-solving technique that was really open to an imaginative generalist, which Edison was, and assumes that problems and solutions have their parallels elsewhere in the field of life.

As he was seeking out someone who could back him to invent more complex duplex telegraphic equipment, he was also experimenting with an electronic vote recorder and a fax machine, originally to tackle the question of how you might transmit Chinese characters by cable. The electronic vote machine was the subject of his first patent but did not go down well with those who might buy it. A state congressional committee reported that it would work so quickly that it would prevent congressmen from organising any kind of filibuster. "If there's any invention on earth we don't want down here, it's this," they wrote. Edison vowed never to invent anything ever again that nobody wanted.

In Boston, he became friendly with another young inventor called Benjamin Bredding, who worked for a promoter called George Stearns, who held the patent for a duplex telegraph. But Stearns sold out to Western Union and neither Bredding nor Edison made any money out of it. Increasingly desperate, but also increasingly determined, Edison made his way to New York, borrowing money to sail there and finish his experiments. When he got there, he bought scientific equipment, skimping on meals to pay for it, was turned down for work and found himself increasingly penniless.

New York was the right choice because there, perhaps more than anywhere else, the telegraph technology was being put to use. It was now used as the primary tool for the collection and distribution of news and other more specialist uses in and around Wall Street, where the growth of financial speculation — something that Edison always disapproved of — found a use for telegraphic printers for the latest prices in a fluctuating market. The moment of opportunity came for Edison in the Gold and Stock Reporting Company, which was devoted to the automatic despatch of gold prices from moment to moment.

The man behind Gold and Stock, Samuel Laws, was also vice-president of the New York Gold Exchange, and Edison got to know his chief engineer Franklin Pope, who liked him and said he could sleep in the cellar until he got to know the equipment and found himself a job.

Then, as so often, Edison had his moment. It came when runners arrived one lunchtime from various brokers complaining that their transmissions had stopped. It was a potentially ruinous disaster for the company and Pope did not immediately know what the problem was. Laws and Pope both lost their heads. But Edison saw suddenly that he could fix it. He saw that one of the nuts had slipped inside the mechanism and he was able to strip down the transmitter to fix it in two hours. Laws offered him a job as Pope's assistant on the spot.

It was a start, but it was to be a bumpy one. The Gold Reporting Company merged with their neighbours and Edison found himself surplus to requirements again. So, three months later, both Pope and Edison set up on their own with the editor of *The Telegrapher* magazine, James

Ashley. They called the company Pope, Edison and Co., and their business was "the application of electricity to the arts and sciences".

That was the spirit of the age. Electricity was not fully understood, but it was absolutely clear to people like Edison that — with the right experiments and the right imagination — electricity could transform the way the world worked, from lighting to transportation. Now the challenge was how to apply it, and here Edison was very quietly, and with increasing confidence, beginning to set the pace.

It is hard to tell now how much Edison's public confidence, which was such a feature of his career and such a driver of his success, was genuine or bombast. He was self-effacing about many things, but he appeared to have absolute confidence in his own ability to solve technical problems. Even in the growing band of inventors wrestling with the issues, he was always certain that he could move the technology on.

He could fix the bugs and make his version the best example anywhere. He always believed he could win the particular races he set himself. He didn't always win, as we shall see, but history suggests he not only knew he could succeed, but that he also knew he would enjoy it. Whatever the truth about Edison's confidence, he soon developed a smaller and cheaper printer, and launched the Financial and Commercial Telegraph Company to market it.

By 1870, it was clear amidst the maelstrom of patents, writs and speculation that the old Gold and Stock Reporting Company was already infringing their patents. Instead of suing for infringement — an uncertain business that Edison tried to avoid for most of his career — they managed to negotiate an agreement with Gold and Stock to develop a new printing telegraph.

It was this agreement that Edison used to pay for office space in Newark in New Jersey to open his first laboratory, the Newark Telegraph Works. From then on, he would never see a contract without adding clauses which would pay for the necessary research.

The three of them had been negotiating with the former chief engineer for Western Union, Marshall Lefferts, the new president of Gold and Stock. And Lefferts was becoming interested in Edison's work. He was particularly interested in plans for a machine that could correct telegraph machines by sending an electrical signal down the wire to reset them.

Pope, Edison and Ashley were still running a private telegraph business called American Printing Telegraph and they managed to persuade Lefferts to grace their letterhead as president too. He then made sure that Gold and Stock bought them out. There then followed the confusion which led to Edison parting company with his colleagues on bad terms — and it was hardly the last time these accusations followed him. Because of their shareholding, Ashley was entitled to $20,000 from the sale and Edison to just $1,200, and Ashley thought even that was excessive.

Edison talked to Lefferts about it and Lefferts advised him to do nothing, then presented him with a cheque when the deal was signed for an extra $1,500. As a result, Ashley banned Edison's name from the pages of *The Telegraphist* and described him as "professor of duplicity and quadruplicity" — a reference to their world of duplexes and quadruplexes at the time.

The speculative world was intervening to make the cutting edge of cable technology even more frothy and complex than before. Western Union had by this time swallowed Gold and Stock under Lefferts, who asked to see Edison. Lefferts asked him how much he thought the sum of all his inventions would be worth. Edison believed it would probably be $5,000 but dared not ask for so high a figure, so he kept quiet. As such Lefferts offered him $40,000 instead and, in astonishment, Edison accepted, (he actually got about $30,000), and he became consulting electrician for Gold and Stock on an annual salary of $2,000. This was more money than he had ever dreamed of, and only a matter of months since he had arrived in New York unsure of when he was next going to eat. He paid off a series of debts and sent money home to his parents — including the original $35 he had borrowed in Boston for his fare to get to New York.

Edison was coming into his own, not just as an inventor, but also as a promoter of his inventions. As always, he displayed huge confidence in his ability to lead a team to develop the best solution possible. He also had confidence that, because they would be the best, he could outcompete anyone transgressing his patents, (at this stage in his career anyway.)

It followed therefore that secrecy was unnecessary, and timing was hardly important either. If he told the papers that he *had* made a breakthrough, then even if he hadn't actually done so, there was little doubt in his mind that he would. He was to change his attitude to patents in practice, though he always disliked dealing with them. Among the many contributions to Edison's career that Lefferts made was to introduce him to his patent attorney, Lemuel Serrell. Ironically, in these early years, he may mainly have been involved, on behalf of his employers, in inventing technical ways around patents to keep himself in the market. And never more so than with the development of the telephone, as we shall see.

Part of the problem for Edison was that, once Western Union had taken over Gold and Stock, which was paying his salary, he found himself working at the same time for the cable giant and one of its main competitors. Then there were his own interests which needed protection, or else all his thought processes would end up owned by his employer.

So, encouraged by Serrell, he began to keep detailed notebooks about his experiments so that he could prove his processes later in court. Multiple projects excited him and helped him make the breakthroughs he needed, but he also needed to carve out some ideas which could later be reserved for himself. The notebooks needed to make clear which ideas were for which employer, and which were for him.

This kind of playing off was absolutely necessary

for his own future and it may, in part, have prompted the remark from Western Union president William Orton that echoed what Edison went on to say about others: that he had a "vacuum where his conscience ought to be".

The new influx of money meant that Edison could set up offices in Ward Street in Newark. For the time being he had a small workforce of engineers, mainly making stock tickers for the various financial offices in New York City, and as always, Edison worked alongside them. He had his own desk in the corner, and his colleagues remembered that, when he had an idea, he would leap up at the desk, swear and do what looked like a Zulu war dance.

What Edison was also doing was improving and improving. There were always tiny ways in which the performance of his machines might be perfected. There were new creations which could transmit automatically, faster than the fifty words or so a human being could transmit and take down. There were machines that printed out using a punched tape. There were facsimile machines and automatic transmission machines, fire alarm systems and other kinds of automatic alarms.

It was at this point, in April 1871 – just as the Paris Commune was forming and the Royal Albert Hall was opening in London – that Nancy Edison died unexpectedly back in Port Huron. Her son's notebooks for the next few weeks remain blank and it seems clear that he was devastated by the news.

When he came back home, there was a new devotion in his life. He had linked up with Gold and Stock to launch a new telegraphic news service, which lasted just two and a half months. During those months, he met and fell for a Newark girl called Mary Stilwell. The moment of committal has gone down in history.

"Mr Edison," she said, as he stood behind her chair. "I can always tell when you are behind me or near me."

There was some light banter between them about why that might be – Edison was, as always, looking for evidence of phenomena – then he said: "Miss Stilwell, I've been thinking considerably of late. If you are willing to marry me, I would like to marry you."

"You astonish me," said Mary, as well she might.

Edison replied that he knew he was taking her by surprise. "But think it over, my dear Miss Stilwell, and talk it over with your mother."

He asked for an answer by "next Tuesday" and they married in Newark on Christmas Day 1871. She was sixteen and he was twenty-four.

It was not exactly an unhappy marriage, but both

sides were disappointed. Mary turned out to have little or no interest in inventing and, although they never separated, it is clear that the couple felt increasingly divided by Edison's workaholism. In fact, the parallel with his relationship with his mother was palpable. Like Nancy, he all but abandoned Mary for his laboratory – for days and nights at a time. She began to suffer from the fashionable nervous complaints of the day, which exasperated him. It wasn't that he was angry or demanding – quite the reverse – he just wasn't there. Within weeks of the wedding, he was complaining in his notebook: "My wife Dearly Beloved Cannot invent worth a Damn!!"

Part of Edison's drive was simply that he needed all the energy and attention he possessed to drink up the available knowledge about each challenge as it emerged, and then to apply that knowledge to ask the right questions to attempt a solution. He was absent because it was his life's mission to wrestle away at a problem, like a puzzle, until it was fully solved. Partly this was also heightened because he was now finding that he had to operate on a more international stage.

At that moment, the pre-eminent telegraphic technicians tended to be in England. This was, after all, a nation which was managing an empire that covered about a fifth of the planet; they needed wireless telegraphy to do so. That was why Edison's main employers, Automatic Telegraph, along with some high profile investors, had been hassling the British Post Office, the government body in charge of the telegraph, asking for the chance to come and demonstrate their equipment.

In 1873, they got their opportunity and sent Edison out to demonstrate their ink recording system. It was his first foreign trip and it was not a good advertisement for sea voyages. His journey on the liner *Jumping Java* was very rough and uncomfortable.

The official tests took place between London and Liverpool. These were unsuccessful also, and Edison believed that this was because the cabling went underground at either end. If they could use a stronger battery, Edison felt, it would work, but the officials were afraid this would destroy the insulation on the wires. They did wonder, however, whether sending more than one message at a time would save them the enormous cost of laying a bigger cable under the Atlantic, so they agreed to organise a test over a greater distance, this time down the 2,000 miles of cable stored in a huge coil at Greenwich, next to the River Thames.

But again, the experiment was not a success. Edison had not encountered the effects of induction before, when wire was held together as a coil. The first dot which came through was printed on his paper, twenty-seven feet long. But while the machine clearly failed to work as intended, Edison's reaction did impress the British technicians. It was clear he had not encountered the induction effect before, but he admitted that immediately and began to think about ways of tackling it. Even more significant was the effect on Edison himself. He realised there were a number of critical things he had yet to learn about chemistry and electrical engineering and was determined to build up his lab capacity in Newark to help him learn them.

It was also the beginning of Edison's remarkably little studied British connection. Within months of coming home, he had gathered together "every conceivable variety of Electrical Apparatus and any quantity of Chemicals for experimentation". He was also aware that British engineers were more familiar with induction than American ones, because they had to deal with submarine cables in a way that his American colleagues were barely required to. He made sure that as many of his manuals and pieces of equipment as possible were written or made in Britain.

By coincidence or by design, it isn't clear which, he also found a right-hand man who was English. Charles Batchelor was born in Manchester and came to the USA in 1870 as a textile mechanic, worked for Automatic Telegraph and then joined Edison in Newark as his experimental assistant, and was his most important number two for the next two decades. Edison kept the patents himself – (in those days, joint patents were open to challenge in the courts) – but he gave Batchelor ten per cent of all their royalties and profits from the equipment they invented together.

Edison's other close associates were mainly Americans, and they included the Massachusetts mathematician Francis Upton and Edward Johnson, who had first hired Edison for the Automatic Telegraph Company. "He ate at this desk and slept in a chair," Johnson wrote later of Edison. "In six weeks he had gone through the books, written a volume of abstracts, and made two thousand experiments ... and produced a solution."

But 1873 was also the year of the economic panic that followed the collapse of railroad companies. In the slowdown that followed, Edison became desperate for money in order to meet his payroll obligations. Facing a crisis, he went to see George Prescott, a senior electrician with Western Union, and offered him a half share in his new quadruplex system, if he managed to invent it. But this agreement didn't solve his financial problems.

The quadruplex was ready the following year, sold by a new company called Edison and Murray. He also began to market a device that administered mild electric shocks as a cure for rheumatism, as well as tackling the fire alarms sold by competitors, working out how he could sidestep their patents so that he could offer those for sale too. But it wasn't enough, and he was soon forced to give up his New Jersey home. He moved his family into a flat above the drugstore near his laboratory in Newark.

It was a scheduled payment of $10,000 to his former partner Thomas Unger which brought financial matters to a head. He asked for his own investors for help and went back to his mentor, Western Union president William Orton. But at a critical moment, Orton went on holiday. Desperately, Edison turned to Orton's great rival, the railway speculator Jay Gould, who had just bought his way into the telegraph world with his purchase of the Atlantic and Pacific Telegraph Company. Gould agreed to buy Automatic Telegraph and to make Edison chief engineer of Atlantic and Pacific, and offered him $30,000 for the quadruplex. To Orton's horror, by the time he got home, the agreement had been signed.

The whole affair seemed to convince Orton in his fears about Edison's conscience. It also led to a huge legal battle between the two men – Orton and Gould – which was only resolved in 1877 when Gould's interests merged with Western Union and they took over the rights to Edison's quadruplex. Edison found, to his surprise perhaps, that he got on well with Gould but that – with no sense of humour – Gould was immune to his jokes and amusing stories, which were such a critical part of Edison's own conversation. He also found, ironically, given what Orton said about himself, that the financial titan's "conscience was atrophied".

Yet there was a distinction, Edison's biographer Paul Israel explained. Edison was interested in money as a means to an end: his laboratory and his experiments. Gould was really only interested in money.

3
Sound

*"They all laughed at Christopher Columbus
When he said the world was round.
They all laughed when Edison discovered
sound."*
Ira Gershwin, 1937

Edison used to claim that his increasing deafness helped him perfect the telephone. Strangely enough, it was deafness which lay behind its development in the first place. Edison's great rival Alexander Graham Bell was exactly the same age, born Alexander Bell in Edinburgh, three weeks after Edison, in 1847.

The whole Bell family was dedicated to the business of improving speaking: Bell's grandfather published a book called *The Practical Elocutionist*, using symbols to show where emphasis should go and where readers should take a breath. It was an early and relatively successful method of tackling people's speech impediments.

Bell's father flung himself into the same cause in London, and moved to Edinburgh with his new wife Eliza, who herself became increasingly deaf, which drove the young Bell on in his interest in acoustics. Bell's father and grandfather forged an alliance and a joint venture in London, inventing a kind of lettering that stood entirely for sounds which would, among other things, allow them to teach deaf people to speak.

Both the youngest Bell's elder brothers died from tuberculosis, spurring a family crisis. Realising that 'Aleck', as he was known, was also weak, his father moved the whole family to Ontario where he believed life would be healthier. In America, he became increasingly fascinated with whether he could transmit sounds electronically.

From 1874, lecturing at Boston University and taking in private pupils – mainly deaf children – Bell had been spending all his spare time and much of his nights conducting experiments in his study in Salem, obsessed with the need for secrecy and increasingly aware that other inventors, more knowledgeable and experienced than himself, were in search of the same prize.

One of them, Elisha Gray, had been inspired that same year by hearing his nephew connect an electric coil to the zinc lining of a bathtub and make whining noises to entertain the children.

The term 'telephone' had, in fact, been coined in Germany in the 1790s and, in July 1874, there was a *New York Times* article describing Gray's experiments sending music by telegraph. "In time," they said, "the operators will transmit the sound of their own voice over the wires."

"It is a neck and neck race between Mr Gray and myself, who shall complete our apparatus first," Bell wrote in November that year. "He has the advantage over me in being a practical electrician – but I have reason to believe that I am better acquainted with the phenomenon of sound than he is." Bell was appealing to the family calling, encouraging enunciation. That was what would give him the edge, or so he believed.

Bell forged an alliance with his wealthy patron and patent attorney Gardiner Hubbard, who had his own reasons – and a long-standing campaign against Western Union's telegraph monopoly – for wanting to discover some other form of communication. The alliance was complicated when Bell fell in love with his daughter Mabel, during his many visits and repeated experiments in Hubbard's house - (Mabel had also lost her hearing and Bell married her once his company was established.)

Bell also fascinated the greatest American scientist of the age, Joseph Henry, then the first director of the Smithsonian Institution, who urged him not to publish the results of his experiments but to press on and complete the discovery himself. Bell complained that he lacked the necessary expertise in electronics. "Get it!" said Henry.

In actual fact, Bell and Gray discovered the basis of the telephone almost simultaneously. That made filing the patent complicated enough, since both were filed almost independently on the same day in February 1876, when Edison was about to move into his new laboratory at Menlo Park, New Jersey.

All this happened before anyone had actually ever spoken through a telephone. That moment came in March, just a few weeks after his patent had been filed, when Bell famously spoke to his assistant Thomas Watson in the next room. "I then shouted into the [mouthpiece] the following sentence," he wrote later. "'Mr Watson – come here – I want to see you.' To my delight, he came and declared that he had heard and understood what I had said, I asked him to repeat the words. He answered: 'You said – "Mr Watson – come here I want to see you".'"

In Watson's autobiography, he said that the breakthrough came because Bell had spilled some sulphuric acid on his clothes. Later on, Bell sang

'God Save the Queen' into the machine. Bell was, after all, still a British citizen.

As soon as 1878, President Rutherford Hayes was installing a telephone in the White House. By then, Bell had set up his National Bell Telephone Company and was beginning the legal battle against the rival lawsuits from as many as 600 rival inventors.

So in the case of the telephone, Edison was not the pioneer. In fact, in this case, Edison was employed by Western Union – just as Bell feared – to circumvent Bell's patent in ways that he was later to accuse rivals of doing to him.

Edison had been asked to look at the telephone by Orton because he held Elisha Gray's patents, though he was also hedging his bets. He was supporting Bell and he wanted to make triply sure by involving Edison too. He sent details of a device involving a pig's bladder developed by a German schoolmaster called Johann Philippe Reis – who was, strictly speaking, the inventor of the telephone – but Edison could not hear it well enough. The sound quality wasn't up to it.

Edison latched onto the problem of how to regulate the variations in the electrical current and put it forward for a patent 'caveat'. Orton was only too aware that, although Bell held the main patent, the maximum range of his phone was only two miles and the two speakers had to shout their conversation down the line. When Bell offered to sell him the patents for $100,000, he dismissed him. "What can we do with such an electrical toy?" he demanded.

Instead, Orton asked Edison to make the invention commercial. In a year of experiments since the famous moment in the patent office, Edison had decided that the solution was to boost the current using the battery he had developed for his quadruplex, and to change the way the main vibrating diaphragm worked – the one that recreated the sound – by including a small piece of carbon. This changed the resistance in the current as the carbon rose and fell under the iron diaphragm.

On 17 July 1877, Edison wrote the word 'Glorious' in his notebook. "Telephone perfected this morning 5.00 am," he wrote. "Articulation perfect, got one-quarter column newspaper every word. Had rickety transmitter at that. We are making it solid."

There was still work to be done on the volume, and the summer holidays to get through, so it was not until September that Edison demonstrated his phone to Orton and his executives, and they put in an initial order for 150 telephones. The following year, there was a test before William Vanderbuilt and Orton over the hundred miles between New York and Philadelphia. It was a huge success. Orton combined Edison's and Gray's patents and set up a company to rival Bell's.

Edison now had a more effective machine, but Bell had an advantage in the marketplace. He held the master patent and, by 1879, the two sides had agreed to call it quits. Orton sold his rights to the Bell Telephone Company and Edison earned $100,000 for his patent rights, which he accepted on the condition that it was paid to him in annual instalments of $6,000. "I saved seventeen years of worry by this stroke," he said later.

In the UK, the rivalry continued until Edison decided he needed to invent his own kind of transmitter so that he need not infringe Bell's basic idea. Once he had managed that, he began to pull ahead in England, aware that there were no telephone engineers there to wire up people's homes.

He recruited sixty of them for intensive training at his new laboratory at Menlo Park and sent twenty to London to start work and to recruit their own local assistants. One of these was the future playwright George Bernard Shaw, who built his experience working for Edison into a novel called *The Irrational Knot*.

"They adored Mr Edison as the greatest man of all time in every possible department of science, art and philosophy," Shaw wrote of Edison's engineers, "and execrated Mr Graham Bell, the inventor of the rival telephone, as his satanic adversary."

Inevitably the two companies merged in the UK and Edison, who claimed to be naive in financial matters, was staggered to receive a cheque for £10,000 when he had assumed it was in dollars - (these were the days when the pound was worth four times the dollar).

It was in these heady days of success that Edison made one of his most important discoveries: how to record sound and play it back. It was a natural successor to his work on the telephone and it came when he had been experimenting with the idea of recording speech on a paper disc. The development of the telegraph had gone in the same direction – first an operator taking down the message and then a ticker tape recording it. So how might you record a telephone message electronically?

An electromagnet with a point connected to an arm travelled over the disk and the signals which came through the magnets were embossed on the disk of paper. If telegraphic signals could be sent at up to forty words a minute, this method could go at the speed of human speech – at over a hundred words a minute. "I reached the conclusion that, if I could record the movements of the diaphragm properly," Edison wrote later, "I could cause such records to reproduce the original movements imparted to the diaphragm by the voice, and thus succeed in recording and reproducing the human voice."

But he rejected the disk idea in favour of a cylinder covered in tinfoil. He made a sketch and wrote $18 on it, which was the extra money he would pay his technician if he managed to make it. Then he gave it to one of his workforce called John Kruesi. Edison took up the story:

"I didn't have much faith that it would work, expecting that I might possibly hear a word or so that would give hope of a future for the idea. Kruesi, when he had nearly finished it, asked what it was for. I told him I was going to record talking, and then have the machine talk back. He thought it absurd. However, it was finished, the foil was put on; I then shouted 'Mary had a little lamb', etc. I adjusted the reproducer, and the machine reproduced it perfectly. I was never so taken aback in my life. Everybody was astonished. I was always afraid of things that worked the first time. Long experience proved that there were great drawbacks found generally before they could be got commercial; but here was something there was no doubt of."

Bell was furious that Edison had beaten him to recorded sound and struggled to catch up. And he would get his opportunity because, for some years, Edison would have his huge energies diverted into what would be the greatest challenge of his life.

4
Light

"Many of life's failures are people who did not realize how close they were to success when they gave up."
Thomas Edison, 1877

In the summer of 1878 – the year of the telephone – Edison went on one of his extremely rare holidays and must have incurred Mary's displeasure by leaving her behind.

The idea was to go to the Rocky Mountains to watch a total eclipse of the sun, and he found himself having a series of what turned out to be transformational conversations with physics professor George Barker, a travelling companion, about the possibility of using electricity to generate light.

The basic principle had been demonstrated with arc lights by Sir Humphrey Davy in the early years of the century, but nobody had cracked the basic practicalities and economics. Arc lights were too hot and too bright. They somehow needed taming and subdividing if they were ever going to be used to light people's homes, and even then there would be problems that had to be solved. There had been experiments in the 1840s using filaments made from charcoal, but they burned out far too quickly.

Edison by then was already a national hero. He had that same year been called "the Wizard of Menlo Park", by one of the north eastern newspapers. So the light problem might have been tailormade for him. He began experimenting as soon as he got home and, five days later, he was unwise enough to unveil his basic idea to the *New York Sun.* His plan was to use a diaphragm to regulate the heat and light to prevent the filament from burning out.

He always managed to project supreme confidence in himself to the press, and there were good reasons for going public to ward off the efforts of his rivals. Whether it had really been sensible to poke the media so early in the game is not clear, but his chat with New York's fearsome reporters did manage to rouse the city's ambitious financial sector to some kind of interest.

Those potential investors who came forward were his long time colleagues in Western Union and also the financial mogul William Vanderbilt. Within a few weeks, they had raised $300,000 and incorporated the Edison Light Company.

The first setback was that the generator provided by a fellow inventor was not efficient enough. Edison responded by designing his own, along with his assistants Batchelor and Upton. Then there was the question of insulation for wire over a long distance. Edison responded by developing a more effective kind. Then there was the bulb itself – the filament, how to produce the vacuum and the right kind of glass to withstand the heat.

The first two of these issues were resolved relatively easily but Edison was left with expensive platinum for the filament and the investors were already getting restive. His techniques for inventing were systematic and successful, but they were not quick. He was pretty sure it needed to be some kind of material based on carbon, but he tested out more than 6,000 different kinds of plants to find the right kind of filament, but nothing seemed to work as effectively as he needed it too.

Edison decided the way forward was probably to inspire the public over the heads of his investors. So on New Year's Eve 1879, he threw open the gates of Menlo Park and invited people in. They found his laboratory lit by 25 bulbs and Edison ready to give a full explanation of the whole issue he was wrestling with. It was small scale but it was enough. The investors stumped up enough to build an experimental generator and the project was back on track.

Perhaps without realising it, Edison was also inventing the modern industrial laboratory. Bell set one up along similar lines in 1881. The Bell Telephone Company did the same in 1883. Edison's biographer Paul Israel explained it:

> "By showing how invention itself could be an industrial process ... Edison helped lay the groundwork of our modern industrial research and development."

He was also reinventing inventing itself. It need not be an individualist series of sudden moments of illumination. It could be a process which, although it might have required a presiding genius at its heart, could massively expand the scope of the original genius and what he or she could accomplish by themselves.

The search for an effective light bulb was an example of Edison's methods at their most intense. And what made the difference was a combination of inspiration from himself and his trusted lieutenants, and the perspiration of learning everything he possibly could about the area he was working in, and then systematically answering all the questions he had set himself.

It was Edison who said that inventing was one per cent inspiration and ninety-nine per cent perspiration.

The key question around light bulbs began to focus increasingly on the question of the filament. Edison could never be quite satisfied. Once he had understood that the longest lasting filament was probably going to be carbon of some kind, probably based on plant matter, then it remained to find precisely the one kind of plant which could work. "I believe that somewhere in God almighty's workshop there is a vegetable growth with geometrically parallel fibres suitable to our use," he told his laboratory staff. "Look for it. Paper is man-made and not good for filaments."

The breakthrough moment was when he had managed to get a filament to burn for 40 hours – because he knew that, once he could get it that far, he could improve it to last much longer.

After finding a piece of bamboo from a fishing rod he increasingly began to focus on the possibilities of bamboo, which seemed to provide the kind of fibres he needed, with no obvious gaps when you looked at it under the microscope. Soon his team were focusing their attention on mandrake bamboo, which came from just one region of Japan. There still had to be an easier alternative to mandrake bamboo.

Edison always understood the importance of public confidence and public spectacle, but there was a limit to what could be achieved by throwing open Menlo Park to the public. The opportunity emerged thanks to one of the most active of their shareholders, Henry Villard, who was also head of the Oregon Railways and Navigation Company. They owned a steamship, *Columbia*, that was fitting out in New York harbour. In April 1880, Villard asked Edison if he could wire the ship for electric light.

It was a wonderful opportunity to demonstrate what he could do, and the development of lighting on board was a huge reassurance for investors. There were no explosions, no fires and *Columbia* set sail for Rio de Janeiro streaming with light. The business of wiring up a single entity like that also meant having to solve some unexpected problems. The first light socket and the first fuse box were both designed for the ship.

But still the search went on. Long after light bulbs were already on the market, the experiments continued. In the spring of 1884 alone, there were another 2,774 recorded experiments to produce stronger lamp filaments which could produce brighter lights and which lasted for longer. Increasingly, the experiments were taking place away from Menlo Park and in New York, where the action was. Edison simply had to be on the spot, so in 1881, he moved to the city and set up the offices of the Edison Light Company at 65 Fifth Avenue.

At the same time, he was thinking about other urban applications for electricity. His assistant Francis Upton was focusing on electric generators. Edison was also supervising the construction of a half-mile scale model of an underground railway system at Menlo Park.

Edison never really developed the electric railway – he thought he was planning electric rail for freight between cities, not light passenger railways for cities, which were eventually developed by Edison's former employee Frank Sprague – who never really got the credit. It was a perennial mistake by Edison to focus too much on the industrial heights of the economy and not enough on the mass market.

Once the *Columbia* challenge had been tackled, it remained to put his vision into effect in New York, and he was already overseeing the installation of a central electricity station there by the end of 1881. But there was still a need to keep his impatient investors on board, so he hit on the idea of wiring up the downtown area around Wall Street. He managed to launch a new company to do it, the Edison Illumination Company of New York. He also launched a company to install lighting in individual homes, the Edison Company for Isolated Lighting.

By the summer of 1882, it was all ready. On 4 September, the directors of the Edison Light Company gathered in the offices of J. Pierpoint Morgan and Edison turned on the switch. The *New York Herald* took up the story:

"The lighting, which this time was less an experiment than the regular inauguration of work, was eminently satisfactory. Albeit there had been doubters at home and abroad who showed a dispensation to scoff at the work of the Wizard of Menlo Park and insinuate that the practical application of his invention would fall short of what was expected of it, the test fairly stood and the luminous horseshoes did their work well."

Edison told his favourite *New York Sun*: "I have accomplished all I promised." It was the crowning moment of his life. There would be other breakthroughs and other triumphs to come, but if there was only one moment for which Edison was remembered by history, it would be this one.

Edison sent Batchelor to Paris to take charge there, and Batchelor shared some of his employer's public relations flair. When their huge generator arrived at the docks, it was given a police escort into Paris and christened Jumbo after the famous circus elephant. In London, they chose Holborn Viaduct as the site for the first central electricity station because they could hang wires under the railway viaduct, which would save time and money. The strategy was going to be different in England, where the regulations were different – parliament wanted energy to be a matter for local government, and the price of gas was much lower. But even there, Edison's assistant Edward Johnson made an impression. "Mr Edison is far and away in advance of all rivals," said the *London Daily News* after Johnson took charge at the exhibition of electric light at Crystal Palace.

It wasn't as if there were no other inventors involved in England. But the only one who really gave Edison pause for thought was the English chemist Joseph Swan. Swan had been experimenting with electric light since 1848 and had also been looking at thin carbon rods in a vacuum, and wrote an account of his work published in *Scientific American* in 1879.

Edison had turned to carbon in October in the same year, so there was an argument about who had come first. Swan's own breakthrough technique involved treating cotton with nitric acid to produce nitrocellulose, in a process involving squirting alcohol through a nozzle.

Swan believed he had anticipated Edison but that Edison had "seen further into this subject, vastly than I." An expensive legal action seemed to loom and, in 1883, Edison's investors forced a merger with Swan United Electric Light Company.

Edison was increasingly cynical about the patent system, and especially in the UK. "The only advantage gained by taking out Patents at all is that you have the privilege of paying a heavy fee to the British Government," he wrote.

By then, he was involved in the other great dispute in the first era of electric light, when both Westinghouse and Thomson-Houston were challenging Edsion's leadership of the industry by using alternating current, which allowed central generating stations to perform at a far higher peak than they could with direct current.

Edison challenged them, not in the courts, but with a public campaign about safety. He was always convinced that AC offered a far greater risk than DC. Only when Westinghouse took it up in 1886 to support electric lighting to smaller towns and villages did he really look closely at AC, and when he looked, he began to have even more serious concerns about using AC at high voltages.

The so-called War of the Currents did not go Edison's way, partly because one of his former employees Nikola Tesla, a Serbian-American genius, left to invent the AC induction motor, which was bought by Westinghouse. Tesla had resigned in 1885 after a dispute with Edison after he believed he had been promised $50,000 if he could redesign the company's DC generator ("Tesla, you don't understand our American humour," Edison had said when he succeeded).

By coincidence, Edison was approached in 1887 by a member of the New York commission to find more humane ways of killing condemned prisoners than hanging. Edison opposed the death penalty but responded to the need to find a more humane way to kill. There was also, coincidentally, an opportunity for a public relations coup against AC power.

After a series of experiments on dogs, Edison's 1888 report found AC the most lethal and concluded that it led to immediate death. His reputation was so high at the time that nobody contradicted him, though actually medical evidence in the 1970s found that electrocution was neither instant nor as painless as his experiments suggested.

What was taking over from his Menlo Park laboratory were the factories producing the various elements necessary for electric light to be rolled out methodically and commercially. This was part of Edison's method. He was not a scientist focusing on a breakthrough, or at least not *just* that; he was an entrepreneur whose attention was focused on creating a whole industry. He was interested in making the different components work separately, so that they could all be improved individually without having to start afresh with a whole new design each time.

What did keep Edison awake in those days, and for most of his career, were his investors. Just as he was generating a great distaste for the whole business of patents, he was also developing a lifelong irritation with financiers. The trouble was that the financiers were too concerned simply with the matter in hand. They wanted him to account for his experiments, and then to scale back the experimentation and to consolidate. He wanted to expand and to think as broadly as possible.

Francis Upton had managed to get the bulbs manufactured for just 29.3 cents each, when enough of them were being ordered. Edison wanted to go cheap to make the technology spread. His investors wanted them to be priced high, so that they could make short-term profits.

Edison wanted to start an incandescent lamp factory, plus an electric tube works and dynamo factory, and he asked his new private secretary Samuel Insull to make it happen. Insull was to be a key part of Edison's British connection. He had joined Edison in 1881 when he was only 20, after Johnson had identified him in London, where he had been working as a switchboard operator.

He arrived in New Jersey with side whiskers, grown to make himself seem older, and was soon managing everything on Edison's behalf, and even buying his clothes for him. Insull was never popular with the staff, probably because he never praised anyone – he "seemed to think that sustained criticism was the most effective spur to efficiency" – but he was absolutely loyal to Edison.

But being useful to Edison was an exhausting business. Insull took to having his catch-ups with his boss when he was ready, which was usually at night. He tended to get down to his correspondence by midnight. It was Insull who found himself at the epicentre of the row with Edison's investors who were restive, once more, this time because they were also concerned and the complex series of companies Edison and Insull had started. Drexel Morgan, one of the most active investors, wanted to consolidate.

The unexpected death of Edison's wife Mary in August 1884 brought matters to a head. It has never been quite clear what she had been suffering from. Their daughter Marion talked about typhoid, but the family doctor makes it clear this was not the case. Instead, he talked about nervous troubles and uterine difficulties. "Seeing my father on Sundays was not enough for mother," said Marion, who remembered Edison sobbing and shaking when his wife died.

The immediate difficulty was that Edison could no longer escape legal action for money owed to a former colleague back in 1874. He had planned to put Menlo Park in his wife's name. Now she was dead, that was no longer possible. It was eventually put up for sale at auction and was bought by Charles Batchelor.

It was also clear that Edison had lost the struggle with his own investors. Henry Villard managed to consolidate all the electrical manufacturing into Edison General Electric, with himself as president and Insull as manufacturing manager.

It was a difficult period for Edison's loyal lieutenants, many of whom did not get the work or the shares or the rights they wanted. This was Edison's reply to a bitter letter from his associate Sigmund Bergmann, who was angry that he would not get the rights to make the new phonograph:

"I have always done everything to help every one of the boys; I have always been glad they were getting wealthy; the more they made the better it pleased me; I am glad you are well fixed; would not do anything to prevent you from making money; all the money you have made yourself through your ability; that you had the chance to exercise that ability was due to me; you have been worked up to a state of dam foolishness by your enemies, of which you have a very choice and extensive collection."

5
Vision

"Anyone sitting in his room alone may order an assorted supply of wax cylinders, inscribed with songs, poems, piano or violin music, short stories, anecdote or dialect pieces. And by putting them on his phonograph, he can listen to then as originally sung or recited by authors, vocalists, and actors or elocutionists. The variety he thus commands, at trifling expense and without moving from his chair, is practically unlimited."

Thomas Edison's grasps how the phonograph will be used, 1888

All this time, Edison had failed to pay attention to the progress of his previous invention, the phonograph, though Bell was catching up. But – as the responsibility for electric light began to shift to the new Edison General Electric company – he began to engage again.

It was on a trip to New Orleans to negotiate with American Bell that Edison first met Mina Miller, the nineteen-year-old daughter of a successful inventor of agricultural equipment, and a pioneer advocate of women's education. They met again in Boston. It was then that he said he had "got thinking about Mina and came near being run over by a street car".

Edison never wasted time agonising about such things and they were soon engaged. Her mother and sister had doubts – Edison was thirty-nine by then – but the men of the family liked him enormously. He always was a man's man. They married in 1886 and went on honeymoon to Cincinatti to see some of his friends from his telegraphic days, and then on to Atlanta. On the way, Edson came up with the idea for an automated cotton picker, which then had to be announced to the press.

The married couple set up home in America's first suburban enclave, known as Llewelyn Park, just outside Newark in a village called West Orange. The house was called Glenmont and had 23 rooms.

Edison was also making notes at this stage about his search for unknown forces, one of which he dubbed the XYZ Force, somewhere between gravity, heat, light and electro-magnetism. He read widely about astronomy. It was also becoming increasingly clear that Edison's main electrical competitor, Thomson-Houston, was winning against his own merged electrical company, because their structure was more streamlined. So early in 1892, the two companies agreed to merge. Their successor was called simply General Electric, with Charles Coffin from Thomson-Houston as CEO, and it is still one of the great corporations of the world.

The negotiations were carried out by Edison's investors Drexel Morgon, whom he regarded as his opponents in the electrical strategy. Drexel Morgan was the entity he feared would finally drag all his efforts down to the short-term narrow instincts of the financiers. They owned a seventh of his electricity company, so they could hardly be ignored. But now, when it came to merging the electrical business, Edison, Villard and Insull were kept entirely in the dark.

At the end of it, Insull moved to Chicago and Edison's greatest creation had spread its wings and flown, leaving him frustrated and cross, but also a very wealthy man. He spent the estimated four million dollars he made from electric light on his rigorous, determined and largely unsuccessful search for new methods of separating iron ore into its component parts. "It's gone," he is supposed to have told a friend later, about the money. "But we had a hell of a time spending it."

Money was not the purpose for Edison. In fact, finance was the tool of an innovative capitalist like him – he needed the money so that he could press on with his innovation. It was that way around. So once the profits from electric light began to roll in, he turned his attention to using the money for the projects he had been dreaming about for years. And the iron ore project had fascinated him: if he could find a more efficient way of extracting raw materials, he felt he could transform the economics of production.

He may have been right, but he was not seeing the changing world as clearly as others would. He tended to focus his attention on big, industrial changes, and was constantly surprised when his innovations were taken up instead by individual consumers. He never really grasped the potential impact of the consumer society, believing that the phonograph would be used for office dictation rather than people playing music – just, as a century later, IBM believed there would only be a market for a few computers in the world.

Nor did he really understand what kind of lives people increasingly wanted to live. His senior staff would willingly work through the night with him on his projects and struggles. They had called him 'the Old Man' since his late twenties. But the junior staff found this kind of one-way relationship difficult. In 1886, he faced a strike in one of his machine works, which may have been exacerbated by Insull's acerbic style.

But what the hiving off of General Electric made possible was a new laboratory, which he built next to his new home in New Jersey. He bought fourteen acres of land on a hill leading up to Llewelyn and asked Batchelor to design a new lab which included a library and a private inventing space for Edison himself. It could, they claimed, "build anything from a lady's watch to a Locomotive". He had high hopes for the new laboratory, planning to use it to develop a new kind of hearing aid, or special ink that could be read by blind people, as well as artificial silk and ivory and a machine for compacting snow off the streets.

Still juggling his investors to find the money he needed for research, the laboratory was nearly ready by the end of 1887. To pay for it, Edison reorganised the Edison Phonograph Company and the Edison Ore Milling Company to find the money, and the Bell Telephone Company paid into the pot for phone research.

Edison deliberately hired generalists, and young ones too, on the grounds that he could influence their development and because they were better at solving problems than specialists. He formed them into teams to take on particular problems, in ways which are still carried on today. Then, like a consultant surgeon every morning, he would do his rounds to see what had been achieved, make suggestions and – although he tried not to criticise – very occasionally to lose his temper. It was a deliberate ploy to encourage a sense of community, aware that this also encouraged his assistants to work long hours of commitment.

The search for better ways of separating the raw materials from iron ore was in this respect a typical Edison project. But it meant tackling huge problems on a scale that he was not quite used to. Even his small, simple equipment had bugs that needed ironing out. The inventing process was, in some ways, a business of solving one bug after another.

There were constant problems. They could barely clean the crusher. It got clogged, then the bricks of raw materials got too wet. He needed to invent solutions to all these problems, one by one, to develop a system of drying, for keeping bricks waterproof, for cooling the wooden pulleys when they ran hot. The wooden equipment had to be recast in iron, and the cost kept rising. The budgets kept rising too and the search for new investors was constant. Edison kept refusing to go public because he wanted to avoid the fatal Wall Street embrace. His project to reinvent the extraction of raw materials was not dubbed 'Edison's folly' for nothing.

To make matters worse, an economic depression swept both sides of the Atlantic, originally triggered by the collapse of Baring Brothers in London in 1890, after over-zealous investment in Argentina. Worse, in 1895, the bricking plant at his Ogden Mine was hit by a strike for more overtime pay, and Edison was forced to abandon work there for two months. When it reopened, there were more problems with dust clogging the machinery again.

The Ogden plant was fully automatic. No humans were involved from when rocks were blasted from the quarry to when the iron ore bricks were loaded onto railway trucks, but it still employed 250 men working two ten-hour shifts.

The whole effort was not without its reward. Edison resolved most of the problems regarding manufacturing Portland cement more easily and cheaply. In 1907, he would design and build a cement house as an experimental way of building economically for the poor.

While Edison's attention had been elsewhere, conceiving of the electrical supply industry and making it possible, the story of the phonograph had been continuing. Alexander Graham Bell had been furious with himself for failing to do for recorded sound what he had done for the telephone. He felt it was his speciality, and he and his team carried on experimenting, rather as Edison had done and would do in the future. It was clear to them that Edison's solution, recording onto tin foil, was not the best way.

It took some years of fruitless experimentation until Chichester Bell, Alexander's cousin, and Charles Sumner Tainter came up with the method of cylinders coated with wax, which would have the recording engraved on them. They patented the idea in 1886 and called the new product the *graphophone*. Then, with the patent under their belt, the Bells and their team came to demonstrate it to Edison to persuade him to have some kind of partnership. Edison was furious, determined to go his own way. "They are a bunch of pirates," he raged.

He asked his faithful British assistant Charles Batchelor to investigate whether wax was really the best material – he decided it was – and struggled to produce his own improved, marketable phonograph, working day and night and closing his laboratory to visitors to give them the uninterrupted time he needed.

The two machines were well matched. But the situation was complicated further by two other developments. In 1887, the inventor Emil Berliner patented his own version which etched a spiral onto a zinc disk, and which he called the *gramophone*. It was then that the successful glass promoter Jesse Lippincott attempted to organise a monopoly of the machines by selling both phonographs and graphophones across the USA.

Lippincott came close to success by negotiating secretly with the team Edison had put in charge of manufacturing his phonograph. Once more Edison was furious and forced to sue his former manager for the return of the fees he had been paid. "The wizard swindled," said the newspapers.

Despite the background noise, the phonograph was pulling ahead of the graphophone, and despite the failure of both Edison and Lippincott to understand what the market for these products was likely to be. The first 'phonograph parlour' opened in 1889 in San Francisco, where customers could order a recording which would then by piped up to them.

Juke boxes operated by coins were beginning to emerge, but still Edison clung to his original idea that his invention was a recording machine primarily for office use. When the Edison Speaking Phonograph Company began it was marketing the instruments along with a special tool to shave the cylinders so that they could be recorded over: Edison was still imagining that he was marketing dictaphones. It was not until 1888 that he began to grasp the real use to which his invention was being put, and there was just time to take on Bell and his other rivals if he acted quickly.

Lippincott died in 1891 and Edison bought his rights and forced the company into liquidation, only to find – in a bizarre legal twist, thanks to legal action by Lippincott's franchisees – that he was unable to use his own patents in the USA for two years. It meant that, for these two crucial years, Edison concentrated his efforts once more on the British market. As a promotional tool, his team there began to record sessions with the greatest men and poets of the age. Even Queen Victoria succumbed (her recording exists but you can't make out what she says).

By 1891 also, and although the phonograph business was driving out competition from the gramophone, the business market for both rival machines seemed to be stagnating. Edison was still set on using his machines in offices or perhaps, at a pinch, as a coin-operated machine in pubs and bars. But the only shops that were actually selling the machines with any degree of success were increasingly finding a use for them in entertainment in the home, and neither model was really simple enough for home use.

As so often with Edison, the circumstances which led him to invent the cinema all came together at the same time. He had certainly been thinking about the possibilities of developing a machine which could do for the eye what the phonograph was doing for the ear, and he wrote a patent caveat along these lines in 1888 – for "the recording and reproducing of things in motion, and in such a form as to be cheap, practical and convenient".

That same year, the pioneer motion photographer Eadweard Muybridge had been lecturing to the New England Society in Orange and demonstrating his *zoopraxiscope*. Two days later, he arrived at Edison's laboratory to talk about combining a series of rapid photographs with sound.

The following year, he was in Paris for the Universal Exposition for the unveiling of the Eiffel Tower – Gustav Eiffel was the "nicest fellow I have met since I came to France," he said. While he was there, Edison heard of the work of the psychologist Etienne-Jules Marey, who had been taking series of photos of animals in motion, using a camera which was able to take 60 frames a second and to print them on a paper-based film. Meeting Marey convinced Edison that what he needed was some kind of paper-based film on a loop.

Edison had already organised a small research team for moving pictures, and he had more urgent projects at the time. There was also no obvious application for this kind of photography at the time. When he came back from Paris, his assistant William Dickson showed him the result of his own efforts.

It used a rotating metal disc and already used sound. Dickson filmed himself raising his hat and saying: "Good morning, Mr Edison, glad to see you back. I hope you are satisfied with the kinetophonograph." Then, to show he had successfully synchronised the sound and pictures, he counted to ten on his fingers.

Edison liked it but was now committed to the idea of a film strip. A year later, he had a result. On 20 May 1891, ten of his new machines were ready to demonstrate. Members of the National Federation of Women's Clubs were holding a convention nearby and were given lunch by Mina Edison, before being shown around the laboratory, where they also saw the first film.

Once Edison had the kinetoscope under his belt, he was once again unsure how it might be used. This looked like turning into the same story as the phonograph all over again, though it was slowly dawning on Edison that he had misunderstood the market for the phonograph.

Writing to his English phonograph company in 1893, he explained that "our experiment here shows that a very large number of machines go into private houses for amusements purposes – that such persons do not attempt to record, nor desire it for that purpose; they simply want to reproduce."

But at that moment, as so often in his career, Edison was confronted by a far more formidable opponent. Lippincott was dead and the rival gramophone was struggling. The new company Columbia took control of what remained of the American Gramophone Company in 1896, and sued Edison to prevent him from using the gramophone patents. It was also clear that the gramophone was also using Edison's patents, so good sense prevailed and they licenced each other to use them.

Edison faced down the new competition with a clockwork phonograph which would play two-minute wax cylinders, called the Home Phonograph. Columbia responded with a cheaper version in 1899 called the Gem. Suddenly, 45,000 people were buying the machines that year.

There was also a battle at the top end of the market. Columbia brought out a bigger version designed for better sound quality. Edison refused to be beaten on sound and responded with the Concert Phonograph. What Columbia understood and Edison did not, was that – once the technology became commonplace and reliable – the real battle would not be over the technology, but over the records or cylinders that played on them.

It was the same story with the new kinetoscopes. They were designed for public places and used a peephole. Once the novelty had worn off, interest began to wane, until Dickson made a half-hearted proposal to try projecting the film onto a large screen. But again, once the technical problems were solved, Edison could barely rouse himself to interest in the films themselves. He backed an attempt to make educational films, but it never quite caught on.

The kinetoscope had reached Europe by 1895 and soon Edison's film studio was turning out over a thousand short films. But the world was changing: Edison's films tended to be of spectacle like acrobats. The world wanted stories and, above all, they wanted comedy and romance.

6

Money

"It is absurd to say that our country can issue $30,000,000 in bonds and not $30,000,000 in currency. Both are promises to pay; but one promise fattens the usurer, and the other helps the people."

Edison on his plan to redesign money, 1921

It was 23 June 1903, in the United States Hotel in Saratoga, New York, when Frederick Winslow Taylor rose to address a meeting of the American Society of Mechanical Engineers on the subject of 'Shop Management'. By 'shop', Taylor meant 'shop floor', as in factory. As far as he was already known to the meeting, it was as a controversial industrial manager who was supposed to have worked miracles of productivity at the giant Bethlehem Steel plant in Bethlehem, Pennsylvania, churning out iron plating for the world's battleships.

The ideas that became 'scientific management' meant breaking every task down into units, measuring how long they take and setting targets for workers to meet. These techniques have somehow broken out of factories, and you can see them working in the new call-centres, and in the service targets, school league tables, sustainability indicators and the battery of statistics by which public services are now run all over the Western world.

By coincidence, at precisely the same time, the car manufacturer Henry Ford was experimenting with the first assembly line as a means to produce his cars far more cheaply than anyone had dreamed of. As far as we know, Edison and Taylor never met. Taylor's obsession with his stopwatch would have amused but ultimately exhausted Edison. But he did feel an enormous affinity with Ford, as co-designer of the modern world. From 1915, he began to take annual motoring holidays with Ford and Harvey Firestone, the tyre pioneer. These were not three scientists out for a jolly; they were three entrepreneurs and pioneer industrialists who could imagine the world differently. On one memorable occasion, President Warren Harding joined them.

When the war broke out, although the USA remained neutral until 1917, Edison was catapulted into the heart of public policy, chairing the Naval Consulting Board, flinging himself into the development of defensive weapons – he preferred not to get involved in offensive ones that could kill – and fighting what turned out to be a losing battle to organise the naval research laboratory along his own lines, employing generalists. Even so, he developed more effective storage batteries for submarines, new ways of producing benzene and ethanol and a number of other breakthroughs.

As peace descended once more on the world, Edison had assumed an almost godlike presence over debate about the future, keeping in close touch with Ford by swapping funny stories. He now had seven children who were out in the world themselves, and his relationships with them were increasingly strained.

His second marriage had undermined his close relationship with his daughter Marion and he refused to lend his son William money for his garage. "I see no reason whatever why I should support my son," he wrote to William's wife Blanche. "He has done me no honour and has brought the blush of shame to my cheeks many times. In fact, he has at times hurt my feelings beyond measure."

Radio was developing fast and as we have seen

Edison never quite understood the idea of consumers driving change. He thought radio was a craze which would not last, but was finally convinced to get involved in the radio market by his sons Charles and Theodore, who were taking increasing responsibilities for the management of the Edison companies. But as it turned out, Edison was right. Without really knowing the Great Depression was on its way, he realised that radio was going to be a cut-throat business. So towards the end of his life, they did get out of radio business.

It was partly because of his friendship for Ford and Firestone, and partly because he was worried about the supply of rubber if there was another European war, that he embarked on his search for an alternative to the natural rubber trade. He also needed rubber himself for insulation material, but the British exercised a monopolistic stranglehold with 70 per cent of the world rubber market. He retired from business in 1927 to find an alternative source.

He eventually chose a rare variation called goldenrod, because it was able to thrive in the United States and only took about three months to reach maturity. Edison believed that developing synthetic rubber would take more resources and time than he had, and its invention had to wait until the Second World War.

Edison had always been suspicious of financiers, believing that they held back progress. He also suspected their attitude to money was self-interested. Edison made a great deal of money in his life time but, as he said, it was hardly for its own sake. "Money isn't the only thing in this mudball of ours," he once told his assistant, Francis Upton.

He also came increasingly to the conclusion that the design of money was wrong, and – in the years immediately after the First World War – he began to think about re-designing it. This was difficult. You could hardly do it in a laboratory; you needed the willing and close attention of the financiers, but they were all off in their own bubble. Yet those years saw a number of scientists and engineers engaged in the increasingly bitter campaign to do the same thing.

People like the aircraft engineer Clifford Hugh Douglas managed to launch a populist movement on these lines, known to the world as *social credit*. The Nobel prizewinning chemist Frederick Soddy was beginning his long, lonely campaign against the Bank of England.

What infuriated the engineers was that the system for creating money had grown up through a series of peculiar, little-understood accretions. Most money was created by banks in the form of loans, to their great benefit and profit. There were advantages to the system in the good times, but – in the bad times – it meant that all money put an inflationary pressure on the economy because the interest on it had to be paid back. There was also a lemming-like panic among banks when the economy turned down. What many of the engineers agreed on was that the world urgently needed a system which was self-regulating – which boosted the economy in the bad times and held it back in the good times, rather than the other way around.

What offended people like Edison was that, if beneficial change had to be mediated by bankers – who could not see clearly beyond their own short-term interests – then the development of the world was likely to be skewed. "Under the old way any time we wish to add to the national wealth we are compelled to add to the national debt," he complained to the *New York Times* in 1921.

Edison was intervening to support his friend Ford's proposal to develop a dam in what were then called the Muscle Shoals of Tennedsee, which they both believed could have a huge productive possibility. It seemed to them insane that they would have to increase the national debt to pay for it. This is how Edison supported Ford:

"He thinks it is stupid, and so do I, that for the loan of $30,000,000 of their own money the people of the United States should be compelled to pay $66,000,000 — that is what it amounts to, with interest. People who will not turn a shovelful of dirt nor contribute a pound of material will collect more money from the United States than will the people who supply the material and do the work. That is the terrible thing about interest. In all our great bond issues the interest is always greater than the principal. All of the great public works cost more than twice the actual cost, on that account. Under the present system of doing business we simply add 120 to 150 per cent, to the stated cost."

What they wanted the government to do was to simply create the money, rather than borrowing it from bankers – and then withdraw the money from circulation when the dam was in operation. "If our nation can issue a dollar bond, it can issue a dollar bill," he said. "The element that makes the bond good makes the bill good. The difference between the bond and the bill is that the bond lets the money brokers collect twice the amount of the bond and an additional 20 per cent, whereas the currency pays nobody but those who directly contribute to Muscle Shoals in some useful way."

Edison became involved in the debate primarily to help Ford. The conversations between the two men had developed the basic idea between them, and Ford took him down to the site of what would eventually become the Wilson Dam, with reporters in tow. The idea they were promoting was effectively that the government would issue zero-interest bonds to finance the dam.

Having been to the Muscle Shoals, Edison began to work more systematically on an alternative plan for money so that its value did not fluctuate so widely – as it was doing in the years after the war. What he wanted to do was to "cast the variable out of money".

He trusted neither the bankers – he called them the "money brokers" – nor a monetary policy based on gold. Britain had been forced off the gold standard during the conflagration, but the United States carried on with what was increasingly a fictional link until the strains of the Vietnam War. But fluctuating exchange rates were even less predictable – and people needed their money system to be predictable.

Edison wanted to get rid of gold altogether – these were the years when the great economist John Maynard Keynes called gold a 'barbarous relic' – but believed it was politically impossible. But he did believe he could underpin the value of money with something real. That was how he came to advocate using a variety of other commodities to back the money supply of the nation.

What he wanted to do was to get the federal government to build warehouses where farmers could bring corn, sugar, cotton, wheat and other crops and commodities and get a cash payment of half the average price over the past quarter of a century. Farmers who did so would also get certificates explaining that they owned the crop. They would pay a small fee to the government for storing the crops for up to a year, then they could either sell the certificates of ownership or use them to get the wheat back. The certificates would fluctuate in value, but farmers could sell them whenever they wanted.

The plan was remarkably like the way they organised money in ancient Egypt, but it isn't clear whether Edison knew that. His main motivation was not just to re-think money, it was also to reduce the risk to farmers so that they could have a guaranteed payment to redeem their loans – and so they would no longer be forced to dump their crops for whatever they could get when it came to the harvest.

But how was he to test the idea? If it had been a machine, he would have carried out his usual experiments on every element. So to try to do the same kind of thing, Edison sent out a questionnaire to seventeen economists – not about the plan as a whole, but about each separate element of it. They included the Federal Reserve chairman William Harding.

The responses were not positive and some of the responses were downright rude – Edison wrote the word 'punk' on one irritable reply. The general critique was that Edison's proposals were expensive and inflationary, and that politicians could manipulate it too easily. Edison believed that they were "in a rut".

Then the questionnaire got out. The agricultural press began to campaign for Ford-Edison money. The plan began to find favour with investors like Bernard Baruch, and radical economists like Irving Fisher. Edison made contact with Herbert Hoover, then Commerce Secretary, but made little progress. The *New York Times* economics columnist Garet Garrett began giving Edison's plan the exposure it needed, but he was hardly supportive either. "Although an extremely able man," Edison replied in a letter to the editor, Garrett "has not got my scheme entirely right in his mind."

Edison quietly withdrew from the debate, but it carried on. Douglas was soon filling stadiums on both sides of the Atlantic, where he had a particular and lasting influence in other parts of the English-speaking world, especially in Canada and New Zealand. Edison turned out to have been right about gold when he predicted its demise. The British found that life back on the gold standard was disastrous, and they soon dropped out again in the financial crisis of 1931.

The idea of commodity-backed money would not go away either, particularly among investors. The doyen of post-war investors, Benjamin Graham, backed a similar idea. Graham was mentor to investors like Warren Buffett, and his 1944 book *World Commodities and World Money* took up many of Edison's themes, proposing that prices be kept stable by a basket of fifteen commodities that were bought and sold on the world market by a subsidiary of the International Monetary Fund.

As for the Ford-Edison plan to finance infrastructure in a different way, to use money as a tool of development rather than to let it wither on the inflexibilities of the big banks, that never happened either. The Wilson Dam was finally finished in 1924 and, by the end, cost $47m. By then, Ford had become obsessed with the iniquities of banks and – in those days – those who believed they were suffering under a conspiracy of bankers were only a hair's-breadth away from believing it was also a conspiracy of Jews, and Ford certainly fell into this fatal trap. Ford was the only American mentioned favourably in *Mein Kampf* and his anti-Semitic newspaper the *Dearborn Independent* gathered over 700,000 readers around the world – though, to be fair to Ford, he always condemned violence against Jews. And, by then, Edison was dead.

Edison's relationship with Mina was more intellectually equal than it had been with Mary. Mina's father had been an inventor too. She understood something of the life, even if she failed to appreciate how much she would have to live with his absence. But they didn't agree about religion.

Ever since reading Thomas Paine as a child, Edison had been a sceptic and he caused ructions in the family in 1910 when he told the *New York Times* that he doubted the existence of the human soul. He also tiptoed into the knotty theological issue of the Problem of Evil. "If he made me," Edison said of God, "he also made the fish I eat."

Mina dealt with this, as she dealt with other divisions, by emphasising Edison's boyishness. In 1913, she described him as this "big smiling, whitehaired, blue-eyed sixty-six year-old boy of hers". The tensions with his children became less fraught as he got older. Theodore was attributed 80 patents in his own right; Charles, who took over the company after his father's death, became governor of New Jersey (Theodore lived until 1992).

Edison always believed in his ability to theorise and to test out his theories with experiment, doubting received wisdom and he particularly doubted the received wisdom from doctors. When he was diagnosed with diabetes in the 1890s, he began to research around the issue. He decided that the problem could be cured with diet, and gave up eating entirely for three years, taking nothing but a glass of milk every three hours. After that, he would supplement his milk diet with some toast, cooked oats, a tablespoon of spinach, a sardine and some biscuits. This was also a diet of a man who hated taking time away from his laboratory.

In May 1931, when he was suffering again – he was eighty-four – he reduced his daily intake from fourteen glasses of milk to just seven and a small orange. He lost a great deal of weight and his intake was barely enough to drive his kidneys. It seems likely that an all-milk diet also made his diabetes worse. In August, he was well enough to go back to his rubber experiments, but soon his kidneys were worse again. By October, his eyesight began to fail and he slipped into a coma. The family gathered around. He died in the early hours of 18 October. He comforted the religious Mina by whispering, just before he died: "It's very beautiful over there."

During his final illness, messages of goodwill had poured in from all over the world. Many newspapers then brought out special Edison supplements. The broadcaster NBC played 'I'll take you home again, Kathleen', his favourite song.

Two days after his death, his body was put in an open casket in the library in his West Orange laboratory, and thousands of people filed past in tribute. President Hoover, as he now was, happened to be away in France for a summit meeting and so his wife was sent to represent the nation at Edison's funeral on 21 October. She sat with Mina and the children in an upper room at Glenmont, the Edison family home, listening to the service being broadcast. Six state troopers kept vigil by his grave for 48 hours.

At 10pm Eastern time, the whole nation turned off their electric lights for one minute in tribute.

7
The future

"The inventor discovers things and the scientist steps in and tries to tell us what it is that has been discovered. The telephone is an invention. Its principle was discovered. Scientists are still endeavouring to tell how it works. We all know it works —that is all the inventor cares to know; but a scientist wants to know why and how it works."

Edison on the key difference between science and inventing

The end of the nineteenth century was a period when people began to extrapolate the future from the trends in technology. It was a time when futurists were hugely popular in the new newspapers and magazines. People adored the stories of Jules Verne or, later, H. G. Wells. But the one that really captured the moment was a book by the utopian socialist Edward Bellamy called *Looking Backward 2000-1887*, which sold more copies than any other book published in

America until that time.

Bellamy predicted the credit card, among other innovations, but otherwise imagined a worryingly rational, authoritarian future, where money was provided to everyone and most decisions were taken by a benevolent government. It was in reaction to Bellamy's militaristic vision that William Morris wrote his own version of this dream of the future in the gentler, elegiac *News from Nowhere* (1890).

But there is no doubt that the new breed of futurists, imagining technological futures owed a great deal to Edison. The French writer Villers de l'Isle-Adam published a novel called *l'Eve Future* where Edison was one of the characters. In 1891, the journalist George Parsons Laphrop asked for Edison's help with story ideas, and 33 pages of the inventors' notes survive. He imagined the manufacture of artificial substances from silk to leather, sending pictures down a wire, aerial transport, single vaccinations, selective breeding to teach humanoid apes to speak English.

Edison never managed to get around to fulfilling his destiny as a science fiction writer, but he remained adept at managing the publicity machinery of the New York media. There he exercised his imagination to predict technologies that would release women from housework so they could reach their full potential, allowing humanity to "reach its ultimate".

But then, Edison's hyperbolic claims did tend to come right in the end. He won the first gramophone battle because he had the resources to keep improving. The film projector was not really his invention, but he argued that it was important to have his name associated with it to guarantee success. His visions of urban electricity largely came to pass. He was an innovator with unprecedented scope (1,093 patents). The famous aphorism by the painter Joshua Reynolds was put up all over his Menlo Park laboratory: "There is no expedient to which a man will not resort to avoid the real labor of thinking".

As the twentieth century went into its second decade, lighting was the development which had the biggest impact on people's lives. But Edison's invention which most thrilled those who encountered it for the first time was the recording of sound. To those who had been brought up at the height of Victorian triumphalism, this seemed like an invitation to immortality.

In the 1890s, when Edison's British representatives were recording all the great names of the age they could persuade, you can hear their astonishment in their short commentaries – invariably that they are "speaking to you now through Mr Edison's extraordinary machine", and that "long after I am dead, people will still be able to hear my voice".

That sense that Edison was somehow breaking the rules of human life, challenging death – just as his electric light had challenged the darkness – was an idea that continued in the science fiction genre. There was just an element of Frankenstein about it.

Looking back at Edison's career, the great successes – the light, the gramophone and the cinema – are familiar shifts of human consciousness. But they are almost less interesting than his great failures, the iron ore project, the re-invention of money and his failure to persuade contemporaries that real innovative breakthroughs are made by generalists and not by specialists.

By the time he died, Edison was himself not qualified to work in any of the rival laboratories that were competing with his own, like AT&T and the Naval Research Laboratory. He had no Ph.D., no specialist knowledge. He was only elected to the American Academy of Sciences in 1927, having been rejected by them the previous year. He was entirely self-taught. He believed, although he might not be qualified to be a researcher, that he had been a success precisely because he was a generalist.

As he said, being a generalist meant he could make parallels with other solutions and ideas. If he reached a dead end in his researches, he could "just put it aside and go at something else; and the first thing I know the very idea I wanted will come to me."

There, if nothing else, is Edison's motto and memorial.

Select bibliography

The leading biography of Edison has to be the detailed and fascinating study listed below by Paul Israel, which I thoroughly recommend. But there are others I found useful in researching this book. They include:

Ronald Clark (1977), *Edison: The man who made the future*, London: Macdonald and Jane's.

Ernest Freeberg (2013), *The Age of Edison: Electric Light and the Invention of Modern America*, London: Penguin.

David Hammes (2012) *Harvesting Gold: Thomas Edison's Experiment to Re-Invent American Money*, Richard Mahler.

Mathew Josephson (1992), *Edison: A biography*, New York: John Wiley.

Paul Israel (1998), *Edison: A life of invention*, New York: John Wiley.

Francis Trevelyan Miller (1931), *Thomas A. Edison, Benefactor of Mankind*: *The Romantic Life Story of the World's Greatest Inventor*, New York: John C. Winston.

James Newton (1987), *Uncommon Friends*: *Life with Thomas Edison, Henry Ford, Harvey Firestone, Alexis Carrel & Charles Lindbergh*, New York: Harcourt Brace Jovanovich.

Quincy Shaw (2016), *Edison*, New Word City.

Randall Stross (2008), *The Wizard of Menlo Park*, Three Rivers.

By the same author: See also...

Scandal by David Boyle

It was Saturday 6 April 1895. The weather was windy and drizzly as the passengers packed onto the quayside at Dover to catch the steam packet to Calais due on the evening tide. Perhaps it was packed that night because of Easter the following week. Perhaps it wasn't as packed as some of the witnesses claimed later, or the downright gossips who weren't actually there. But it was still full. Those waiting on the quay wrapped up warm against the chilly Channel breeze and eyed each other nervously, afraid to meet anyone they knew, desperately wanting to remain anonymous.

Among those heading for France that night was an American, Henry Harland, the editor and co-founder of the notorious quarterly known as *The Yellow Book*, the journal of avant garde art and writing which had taken England by the scruff of the neck in the 1890s. Harland had come to Europe with his wife Aline, pretending to have been born in St Petersburg and planning to live in

Paris, but had instead made his London flat, at 144 Cromwell Road, the very hive of excitement in the literary world. Henry James, Edmund Gosse and Aubrey Beardsley came and went. The parties were talked about with awe and excitement. Henry and Aline always spent the spring in Paris, so they were not leaving the country suddenly and in desperation, but it dawned on them that the reason the quayside was so packed that night was because many others were.

The name of the ferry the Harlands boarded has been lost to history. It was probably the *Victoria* – her sister ship the *Empress* had been badly damaged in a collision the month before and was now in dry dock. There she heaved beside the sea wall, as the muffled passengers filed up the gangway, her twin rakish masts and her twin funnels belching smoke, her two paddlewheels poised to drive across the world's busiest sea lane at 18 knots, her stern flag flapping in the wind with the insignia of the London, Chatham and Dover Railway.

Harland had a good idea why the ferries were full, though he was still surprised. He was also aware of at least some of the implications for himself. Oscar Wilde was arrested for 'gross indecency' that evening, having lost his libel action the day before. The news of the warrant for his arrest was in the evening papers, and included the information that Wilde had been arrested while he had been reading a copy of *The Yellow Book* (this was quite wrong, in fact; he was reading *Aphrodite* by Pierre Louys). Harland could only guess the motivations of those who were now suddenly crowding across the English Channel, but it looked remarkably like fear. They huddled in corners in the stateroom downstairs, out of the wind, damp and smuts, wondering perhaps whether they would ever see their native land again.

There was an unnerving atmosphere of menace that evening. One item in the evening papers implied that the nation was perched on the edge of a scandal that would make the establishment teeter. "If the rumours which are abroad tonight are proved to be correct we shall have such an exposure as has been unheard of in this country for many years past."

Did it mean the exposure would reach those who run the nation, or did it mean something even more terrifying – that the exposure would spread downwards through society? As the passengers new only too well, the combination of events which they had feared for a decade had now come to pass. It had been a few months short of ten years since the so-called 'Labouchère amendment' had been rushed through the House of Commons, criminalising homosexual activity of any kind between men. It was never quite clear why women were excluded – there is no evidence for the old story that Queen Victoria claimed it was impossible. For ten years now, they had watched the rising sense of outrage at the very idea of 'homosexuality' – though the term was not yet in common use – and had realised that there might come a time when that law was enforced with an unsurpassed ferocity.

It wasn't that they necessarily had anything to be ashamed of – quite the reverse – but they had reputations to be lived down, some event in their past or some 'unfortunate' relationship behind them. Now that public concern had turned to what looked like public hysteria, they clearly had to be vigilant. They did not want to be accused, as Oscar Wilde was accused, by a violent aristocrat of doubtful sanity, and would then have to respond in the courts or the press. They could not face the fatal knock on the front door from a smiling acquaintance who would turn out to be a dangerous blackmailer.

But now the unthinkable had happened. Wilde had been stupid enough to sue the Marquess of Queensberry for libel, and had lost. The public had driven each other into a crescendo of rage and it seemed only sensible to lie low in Paris for a while. Or Nice or Dieppe, or the place where the British tended to go in flight from the law – Madrid. Anywhere they could be beyond the reach of the British legal system.

As we shall see, one of those who fled, as I discovered during the research that led to this book, was my own great-great-grandfather – escaping for the second time in a just over a decade, in a story that my own family had suppressed for three generations.

**

It is no small matter to flee your home and go abroad, especially to do so within the space of a few hours to gather your belongings and make arrangements for your property or your money. As it is, escape was only a solution available to those wealthy enough to flee. It is even tougher perhaps for those in some kind of unconventional relationship, ambiguous to the outside world – but perhaps not ambiguous enough – aware that the decision to go was probably irreversible. It might look like an admission of guilt.

On the other hand, what could happen when the newspapers could unleash this kind of bile? What would happen when they had successfully gaoled Wilde with hard labour and turned on his friends, and anyone else who looked unusual? What would happen if the rumours were correct and the scandal would shortly engulf the government and royal family? Harland did not know at this stage that, when the news about *The Yellow Book* became clear on Monday morning, a mob would gather outside the offices of his publishers Bodley Head, and would break all the windows. "It killed *The Yellow Book* and it nearly killed me," said publisher John Lane later.

We know now that, in the event, the threatened conflagration did not take place, but in the remaining 72 years while Section 11 of the Criminal Law Amendment Act, the Labouchère Amendment, stayed on the statute books, 75,000 were prosecuted under its terms, among them John Gielgud, Lord Montagu and Alan Turing.

Many thousands of lives were ruined – Turing committed suicide not long afterwards, having been forced to undergo hormone treatment that made him grow breasts.

Yet that moment of fear in Britain in 1895, unprecedented in modern times, has been largely forgotten. It is remembered as a sniggering remnant of gossip, about the number of English aristocrats or others in public life, living incognito in Dieppe, or glimpsed in the bars in Paris, and the awareness as a result that they had something to hide. One of the purposes of this book is to remember it for what it was – one of the most disturbing chapters in modern English history, when public horror at sexual behaviour reached such intensity that nobody seemed completely safe, and nobody could be relied on to protect you. And when a man like Wilde, the darling of the theatre critics, with two sell-out shows in London's West End theatres, could be brought low by a furious, litigious pugilist – well, really, who was safe?

This unique moment of fear in English history came at a peculiar moment, at perhaps the apogee of tolerance in so many other ways – women were cycling and getting university degrees, training to be doctors. Mohandas Gandhi was a London-trained barrister working in South Africa. George Bernard Shaw was overturning assumptions about the right way to dress, eat and spell. H. G. Wells was sleeping his way through the ranks of the young female Fabians. Edward Carpenter, in his sandals, was advertising freedom from the constraints of conventional sexuality, having forged a gay relationship with a working class man from Sheffield. William Morris was still, just, preaching a revolution based on medieval arts and crafts. And yet the rage at the idea that men should love each other sexually threatened to overwhelm everything.

That morning, Queensberry had received a telegram from an anonymous supporter, which read: "Every man in the City is with you. Kill the bugger."

Why did it happen? Partly because of growing public concern following the Labouchère amendment, sneaked though Parliament in 1885, but even that was more than the individual brainchild of a lone radical. Why this shift from tolerance of the changing role of women and emerging new ideas to this threatening public rage? How did homosexuality emerge as a key issue in English public life?

The answer lies in the events that took place in Dublin a decade before, starting with the political aftermath of the murder of Lord Frederick Cavendish, the son of the Duke of Devonshire and the newly-appointed Chief Secretary to Ireland.

**

But I had a more personal reason for finding out the answers to some of these questions. My family lived in Dublin in the 1880s. The reason that they don't any more, and that I was born in England not Ireland, was because of those same events there in that decade. Until the last few years, when I began researching this book, I was unaware of those events.

All I knew was that my great-great-grandfather, the banker Richard Boyle, had left Dublin suddenly and under a cloud around 1884. His photograph has been torn out of the family photo album, with only his forehead remaining. There are no likenesses of him anywhere that I know about. The letters related to these events in the family, and what followed, have long since been destroyed. I believe I was even there when my grandfather burned the last of them on the bonfire around 1975.

I had always been interested in what might have happened, but had assumed that the memories were now beyond recovery, just as the fate of my great-great-grandfather was lost in the mists of unfathomable time.

As it turned out, I was wrong. I was working on another incident in Irish history in the British Library, and discovered as I did so that a whole raft of Victorian Irish newspapers had been digitised and were now searchable online. On an impulse, I put in the name 'Richard Boyle' and searched through the references in the Dublin papers. Then, suddenly, my heart began beating a little faster, because there it was – the first clue I found to a personal tragedy, and a national tragedy too: this was the spark that lit the fuse which led to the criminalisation of gay behaviour and the great moment of fear that followed the arrest of Oscar Wilde. That first clue led to others, which led to others. I will never know the whole story. But what I did discover took me on a historical rollercoaster, and an emotional one, which catapulted me back to the strangely familiar world of the end of the nineteenth century – and a glimpse of that sudden fear in April 1895 that drove many of those affected so suddenly abroad.

See *Scandal: How homosexuality became a crime* (www.therealpress.co.uk)

Other books by David Boyle published by Endeavour and the Real Press...

Fiction
Leaves the World to Darkness
Regicide: Peter Abelard and the Great Jewel

Non-fiction
Toward the Setting Sun: Columbus, Cabot, Vespucci and the Race for America
On the Eighth Day, God Created Allotments
The Age to Come
Unheard, Unseen: Submarine E14 and the Dardanelles
Alan Turing: Unlocking the Enigma
Peace on Earth: The Christmas truce of 1914
Jerusalem: England's National Anthem
Rupert Brooke: England's Last Patriot
Operation Primrose: U110, the Bismarck and the Enigma Code
Before Enigma:
Codebreakers of the First World War
Lost at Sea: The story of the USS Indianapolis
Dunkirk

HOW TO...
books from
the Real Press

How to become a freelance writer

This is a manual about freelance writing with a difference. It won't tell you how to write or what to write. It assumes you know these things already. It doesn't set out to equip you for a brief period of freelancing.

It will, on the other hand, tell you how to go about living a writer's life in a practical way – how to plan ahead, how to shape your career, how to find clients and how to deal with the money. It will tell you how to make a life out of writing without falling into the many little traps that are set for us once we embark on the idea.

If you are thinking of changing your life, you may be tempted to buy many other books about how to write, or taking the first technical steps into becoming a freelancer – but this book will set you on the path to live that life.

www.therealpress.co.uk

25740723R00073

Printed in Great Britain
by Amazon